More Near-Ghazals (151-200)

Dan Giancola

ISBN: 978-93-6354-049-1

First Edition: 2025
Rs. 200/-

Cyberwit.net
HIG 45 Kaushambi Kunj, Kalindipuram
Allahabad - 211011 (U.P.) India
http://www.cyberwit.net
Tel: +(91) 9415091004
E-mail: info@cyberwit.net

Printed at Repro India Limited.

151

Dawnlight like dishwater rinses dark   wakes me
Drizzle lacquers with aqueous layers the steaming snow

Frogs float in a vernal pond   cluck like chickens
Best to chill & get the chill out

Pleasantly adrift I seldom feel home at home
Wind chimes wheeze   crocus glow like candy

Mourning cloak shadows float the path before me
scouting eternity   I'm learning my way there

Another whisky   Barkeep   You have one   too

152

Another mistaken reality   stove in horse
-shoe crabs   helmets of slain warriors

Above nests ospreys with the wind dance
I struggle to write my next sentence

No closure   No resolution   Such concepts
belong to youth & those never neglected or left

No justice without victims but no one's
victim who grants forgiveness   Be the cheek that turns

No meaning has any worth   Dan   but your own

153

Shrouds slap a mast   keep bay's pulse
until Time crumples into one note *Now*

Freedom releases us from certainty
We grow when we *don't* know

Pelicans like angels skim waves wind herds
toward their explosive evanescence

The ethics of perception require a stay
from fear & intimacy with the unexpected

I approach & birds in your eyes startle

154

Insecure about your insecurities   you fail
to embrace the silence with which we are made

Margaret Fuller strides Point-O'-Woods tides   sea
-lettuce petticoats & fish-bone stays rank with life

Distant fish stakes pin haze to bay-chop
The tailor left for lunch but his seam never wavers

To the table you gave me thirty years ago   Tom
bring the flowers that sprout from your bones

Not much   memeifying quanta   transposing the *Geist*

155

You stand in your decadence like a cheap used suit
poised between dissolution's start & rot's ripeness

Imagination embedded in love's wasted attenuations
results in storms without rain   tears without pain

The devolution from hippy to yuppy is not
inevitable   Guard your ideals against despair

Two drunks asleep on the park's lawn
are still believed to contain water

C'mon   Dan   do something subversive

156

Anything more American than grifting & lynching
more than the land-grab, litigation, tax on bread

Why can't we know one another   why
has our solitude deepened with our privacy losses

When will we think ourselves beyond the Bible
divest ourselves of that destructive delusion

Where will you be when earth like a rabid dog
turns against us   how reverse our profitable failures

Who will vint the final party's apocalyptic wine

157

Do individuals exist   Does a dream dictionary
prove our inner lives identical

If I tell you what you want to hear   will
you reply with silence   our true currency

Can I invest my love like money   watch
it compound & grow   Where's that high-yield CD

Do artifacts strewn in your life's debris
field result from indifference   love   or pride

Can I bend the world to my vision or will it twist mine

158

We spin truth today like cotton candy
Sweet   yes   but lacking nutritional value

Love particles form gravitational waves
in which we often lose ourselves & drown

I miss intimacies   limbs entangled like quanta
igniting ecstasy's vigor & its revelations

Somewhere across space & time the light
that illuminated our togetherness projects its images

She said   Dan   love's forever but not always yours

159

With no belief in permanence   why
drop an anchor in lapsed time with a tattoo

Wind   never still   sweeps clean
& sends on its way all the hobo trash

With every breath the world begins anew
Each heartbeat commemorates a world reborn

Babies bawling at the wake
remind us life & death are always one

Time grows in the grape   We sip sun in our wine

160

Morning-glory's white trumpet goes mauve
about the bell bruise beginning the blues

Early evening yellow August stormlight
begins to pink We stand inside a flower

She'll cry a few minutes when you die daub
damp cheeks with a wadded Kleenex & move on

Waves roll ashore as relentlessly as days
roll off calendars each different each the same

Sorry Dan The wine's gone Whiskey

161

Not for a second do I believe a single
thing you tell me despite your model's smile

From an ashtray a blue mud dauber harvests last
year's rain fallen last night for this year's nest

You're convinced tinnitus is the universe whistling
time from the heart of silence slipping

Don't threaten me with your next too soon
doomed technology   The striped bass are biting

Uncage the birds in your throat & give us a tune

162

The waxing moon exhausts itself
all month searching for its other side

Unsustainable   the moment after
a stubborn knot you've battled loosens

Cattail shadows calligraph an alphabet
on asphalt &   swaying   write wind's libretto

Reality does not exist   the grad student said
about to plunge his hand in molten lead

Taste the moonlight   Dan   that honeys your whiskey

163

House too small   sky too large
too empty   Where do I fit in this world

Vines tendril emptiness above   climb ser
-pentine air stairs looking to strangle stars

In moonglow we know eternity's now
lose count of hours that bind us to time

For one night white moths swarm   revolve
pheromone melodies   look to breed not love

You're a flesh-cask   Dan   where wine finishes its howl

164

Barges rust below a cauliflower sky
& fog blindfolds a pond's lidless eye

Pelicans like littered paper or grey-white
brushstrokes glide below a solstice sundog

A storm smudges the coast   You watch
closely to keep your heart afloat

Who says she's no poet who follows her
satchel of sad broken poems into a river

A fly scouts a tiled floor's salt-flat waste

165

Sunlight sleeps this morning in grass-top webs
silver hammocks sagging with emptiness

Spider webs like opaque erasures in the grass
blank cosmological reports   author unknown

Grass spiders' webs like turned-out
pockets attest to poverty's hungers

Along a tow-path this morning webs appear   pro
-paganda leaflets whose importunings sun bleaches

Be-dewed webs take shape like spirits under sheets

166

Dotting like poppy seeds a distant slope
beeves browse   Above   buzzards bide time

I chase day west & night chases me
toward the horizon   thin & yellow as old paper

I'm tired of women who just want to be friends
Where's she with whom I might twine my soul

Gorgeously inhospitable   Eagle Canyon glows
Ah   the aridity of beauty without love

I float on fumes from the wine of your voice

167

In fall's Arizona creek-beds water ghosts
purl above flows of warm gray stones

Before *cerros rojas* & along a solar-panel lake
a three-engine freight train enters the moon

Driving up past Chilili toward Quarai   frost foils
junipers & pines   tailings mined from morning's shaft

Crows like shards of night scan silted washes
for voices lost to dawn-exploded dreams

You want to be formless & everywhere   Dan   like sunlight

168

In her palm a woman cradles her phone   balletic
fingers slender as egrets choreograph a text

Sleeping on a train in her hijab   a woman
pillows her head with a leatherette Koran

From beneath her bonnet a Mennonite teen
dares me to stare into the knives of her eyes

I watch a station-drunk who can't find her
wallet hand out Sweeties with a bloody face

She might appear anywhere   like luck or tragedy

169

Between banks the Terrell River lies   pewter-blue
stroke laid-in with a clumsy painter's palette knife

A raft of brant nudges shore   Do they know
where they are   where they'll need be tomorrow

A week passes   You've done nothing but eat & sleep
piss & shit   your life a velleity   Who are you

The Terrell River's mouth spews a moraine
speaks in silt & gravel   grumbles erosion's deposition

Think again   Dan   She won't arise from your need

170

Night's tide floods sky with fish scales & Venus
on its tether swings around the mooring of the Moon

You've been wounded in the war with love
you lost   don't feel joy the way you used to

Beside a pool cover puddle a red-tailed hawk blinks
a finch in a talon twisting to sip its own drink

What incubations within percolate   gestations
inchoate   *seemings* eternal   what fire & frailty

Be a man of action   Dan   Go take a nap

171

Drizzle inundates a fog that tinsels night
Gray boredom becomes stasis   stalls

A kid   I'd watch time move   clock's
minute hand with glacial *thunk* tock

Looks at me like she doesn't know me
watching all her prior selfies in my eyes

My 775th full moon smolders   brief illusory
paralysis that   rising   shrinks into a chad

Be the whiskey nip that tips my equilibrium

172

Your call is important to us   Your call
will be answered in the order received

Please continue to hold   Your call is important
to us   Your position in queue is two

Please wait for the next available agent
Your call will be answered in the order received

Your call is important to us
Your position in queue is two

Please continue to hold

173

Sirens a week before Christmas tell our good luck
Santa's in town slinging candy from a fire truck

In winter chill the homeless convene their carts
rub hope   that faint warmth   into hands & hearts

We're all of us just one bad break
from living on the street   Enjoy that steak

I must for so much atone
so when I weep I weep alone

O how your wine-stained tongue makes me groan

174

Exposed to truth   gilt with which we gild belief
will tarnish   Stubbornness revives the luster

Trying to preserve its dignity   Ignorance
cites lies   doubles-down on stupidity

Believe what you'd like but don't force
everyone else to accept your fallacies

Because a truth is not a friend to you
in no way makes that truth untrue

Don't sell as wine what we know is vinegar

175

In the moment you don't know how you know
what you know   see no future beyond an hour

Many years she loved me   Then not   Spring
has not yet returned to this nanoplastic heart

What would you do for the spoonful of immor
-tality given the minor poets' most minor poet

Cezanne-like semiotic rain-makers heave
into view & stall   All day we wait to read the rain

Toast your blood   Dan   & all else that fails you

176

Your personal information has been stolen
so often you feel like a wrongful conviction

Faucets with dry rotted washers   my kidneys weep
drip by drop indifferent protein tears into my pee

Atop a pole against half a daytime moon
a mockingbird trills convivial ringtones

Adept at rationalization   America may yet
elect a sex offender   traitor   fraudster president

Peeling garlic   lost in the time beyond time

177

Distant thunder someone rummaging
through a cooler filled with ice & beer

My knife enters a pepper's hollow
where silence broods over the nothing it rules

What happens when the one you're meant
to be with is not meant to be with you

I stone an avocado
Are you there Emptiness

Let's hike together zero's icy trail

178

I keep my private life private   Digits don't
count   only the poems I will never write

Today my mind's a foreign country   a strange
tongue's words a currency I can't exchange

Do I still believe in love   Nothing I've read
seen   heard   or lived of love anymore seems true

Bills paid   Happy to stay home   sauté
peppers   garlic   & sardines for pasta sauce

Six ounces of wine   Dan   suffice to scrub the buds

179

You once preferred Art to Life   Now old
the irrelevance of eternity you understand

If our brains say *take the escalator*
& we opt for stairs   what do we obey

Half spring all winter   cloudy low forties   sunny
low fifties   No snow   The robins never leave

A stub vouches   Of the show no
detail remains   Did you really go

Brushing your teeth you picture your grave

180

Toward dawn darkness drains
blues like a drunk's varicose nose

What good does it your heart going out
to victims by unknown gunman shot in the heart

Sunrise spills across the sky like puke
morning slick & fetid as a barroom floor

More mass shootings than days this year
No one free who fears a public bullet

No one today at the bar orders shots

181

There   in the steaming center
of the yam I butter   infinity

How could we ever not have lived on be
-coming's endlessly scrolling   iterative loop

Out walking I come across a cat not long
dead   fleas making psychedelic music in its fur

Moment to moment I live a life I neither
understand nor hope to   its mystery my balm

Glimpse the future   watch the past grind into view

182

Walk into any house after fish fry   catch
the tang of burnt light   low tide   soiled diapers

Few things more dismal than February rain
Politics   sure   & our penchant for murder

A cedar's green freezes   ochers   limbs
sagging with snow they embrace like a lover

Hoist from the dark well of consciousness
Now's urgent sounds   Although you can't   sing

To cure reason I quaff the moon afloat in my wine

183

Even steam jigs shadows on the kitchen floor
When the tea water boils   I dance

You are *a definite indefinite* you say
Like death   I ask   *unexpectedly expected*

In their viduity women have given me their retro
virginity   never their shy   armored hearts

My guts purl & gurgle   Listen   biome music
microorganisms singing whale songs

I live simply here   Bring your own glass

184

3 March   Seventy degrees   An amphibian
symphony & turtles taking sun like teenage girls

It's not you   it's me   you say   the cliché
blunting the blade you slide between my ribs

Springing into daylight savings time
my car's clock is once again correct

A tick ascends hair by hair my leg   Why
does it stop *just there* to gnaw my thigh

Don't toast pursuit of a life for which you've no talent

185

I spend the day before vacation jonsing
to go   mind raking leaves in a hurricane

In D.C. we switch from diesel to electric
engine   in minutes moving through centuries

Some places I've lived are no more
No more does the person who lived there exist

Sliding by along the track   the abandoned   derelict
American Dream   rusted beater sinking in sod

It's only *self*   Dan   as fickle as love

186

Travelers at the station bid loved ones farewell
I guess at those who will not meet again

Last night I slept in your mouth eavesdropping
your dreams   your breath a warm throw

Where begins intimacy   Some say touch   some
talk   some the revelations of a curbside mattress

We repeat our lies until they build beliefs
Welcome to the post-veritas apocalypse

In the wine   nose it   becoming's putrescence

187

A yellow finch bright as a doubloon darts
into a shrub & disappears   puts out the sun

Spring's a mud room where cherry trees lift
lacy prom dresses so as not to stain their hems

A swamp rill chuckles as I leap it   then   hiking
uphill   I hear fallen leaves applaud the rain

Your recorded voice never sounds like you
& what you see in mirrors is not what others see

Trust wine's insights when you can't trust your own

188

Seismic rumble   House shakes as if with chill
I in it as after news of a loved one's death

Not much razzle dazzle outside totality's path
just someone's thumb smudging the sun

Through eclipse glasses the sun looks like an oxy
Day darkens   Shadows lengthen   A chill descends

Earthquakes   eclipses   suspicious
of auspiciousness   I watch bread mold

Holy-rollers want repentance   Give them science

189

Poor moon   earth's only child   wallflower
pale & pocked   who will ask you to dance

Don't fall in love with anyone
in the process of becoming someone else

Intuition aside   we don't know until
we know that love fades or organs fail

Wind moves reflections of flooded trees
dance of object & image   Am I moving or still

Time again   Dan   to change your life

190

I like poems with no subject but themselves
working hard like people to discover who they are

Daffodils nod on the Forge's bank   cool stars
in river's green sky   not sensing their nature

The universe's a sepulchre into which time
collapses   but *now*'s timelessness & never lapses

Like a poem about poetry   self-conscious   in
-dulgent   insecure   I struggle to understand myself

In the black holes of her eyes I watch time die

191

Spring snow swirls I wonderingly stare
Each flake with precision falls *there there & there*

Radio preachers bless airwaves across the nation
Jesus everywhere except in people's hearts

Oak crowns brush sky's gessoed canvas
with the yellow curry of their buds

Off a path deer bound into undergrowth & vanish
join again the world beyond our senses

On your lover's lashes Dan demodex teem

192

After an orgy of berry gorging   robins disappear
plucked stems like skeletal hands clutching air

Like hyenas on a carcass   people stare
one another down for the last evicted curbside chair

Drop a body in the sea   writes Robert Cushman Murphy
& isopods clean its bones until with museum quality they glow

All that's left of love   photos that fade in albums
like sarcophagi   a voice waning in the wind of time

Moon shines tonight like a newly shorn head

193

Gray all day rain   Inside   a sleeping dog's legs
swimming to keep from drowning in a dream

Gulls like voracious shadows in sunset relief
devour daylight   bodies like black blades flashing

Because we've ruined their futures   we've no
right judging subsequent generations' sensitivities

I think of my poems then come to my senses
know my immortality lies in the U.S. census

Nothing   Dan   Nothing is as it was

194

Stack logs beside a gas fireplace to complete
an illusory tableaux   no smoke   no creosote   no heat

What obscures the highway's horizon isn't haze
but a cloud of pollen like urine-soaked gauze

A lunar halo's pale hues circle my irises
auger illness   struggle   days full of crises

No one anymore rings bells for vespers
Taped tintinnabulations slur like blurred whispers

What we don't know   Dan   is always with us

195

Most suburban homes oppress their owners
with upkeep's tyrannies & totalitarian lawns

Anything less delicious than a Red Delicious
Call an abhorred job joyful trusting suspicious

Moving will only exchange the loneliness I feel
among friends for the loneliness I feel alone

The common blue opens its wings a chip of sky
like a screen on which I watch my past scud by

Wine does no good in its bottle Release its dreams

196

All my life I've waited for the words "You're
dying" Silly me I've been dying all my life

To see the not-keen-to-be-seen balm
of every birder sea explorer peeping tom

You see it's just like I've been tellin'
That fascist Trump is also now a felon

A spider's silken thread streams from the aft
stay invisible sail's foot luffing in sunflow

From a lover I long to hear *I love you* & it be true

197

Down block dogs snarl   yowl   bark   Tearing apart
a stranger or pack leader's back bearing an enemy's heart

You see faces in leafy crowns entangled
Wind shifts shadows & an old man winces

Sun's hot iron presses into skin humidity
I wear like laundry steam   wet sheets hanging in my eyes

Nothing makes me happier nowadays than a low
blood pressure reading (used to be whiskey's glow)

The spirit's deep-state   Dan   undermines your will

198

What has mass a river moves Not my
reflection illusion of a self itself illusory

Pollen & humidity combine to gild an afternoon
Liquid hours slide by wearing citron auras

Every day entropy is winning Doesn't matter
what we do the world prefers to fall apart

Sometimes I feel the universe wrap me I am
quanta & the dark matter between stars

In wine we find understanding Drunks die of it

199

A sparrow on my deck-rail sits zazen   Pre-flight
it stretches a wing   old man rising from his zafu

Days after the Fourth   far-off fireworks rumble
colorless drums evoking silent illumination

A friend asks   Is love an illusion   No   love's dopamine
flooding your brain when she enters the room

We malign those with whom we don't align
Only shared perspectives keep us coupled

Photons fidget   Spacetime flexes   We flux

200

Do what you must to avoid routine   that sleep inducer
enemy of accidents that evolve joy from emptiness

Fireflies penetrate a cling-wrapped trap   drown
in apple vinegar   circling wakes whirling them down

Nothing lasts   nothing disappears   nothing returns
Raspberries don't care   plump rubies on arching canes

How shallow the self & its tenebrous vacancies
magician's prop sustaining the illusion that we matter

Hoist a glass of starlight   Dan   & toast the void

www.ingramcontent.com/pod-product-compliance
Lightning Source LLC
LaVergne TN
LVHW091237150826
845673LV00003B/1190

* 9 7 8 9 3 6 3 5 4 0 4 9 1 *